Especially for

....

From

....

Date

....

GOD IS IN THE SMALL STUFF

Family Advent Devotional

Invite God into the Details of Your Christmas Preparation

BRUCE BICKEL & STAN JANTZ

SHILOH RUN 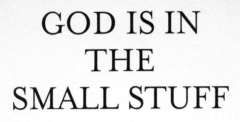 PRESS

An Imprint of Barbour Publishing, Inc.

Published by Shiloh Run Press, an imprint of Barbour Publishing, Inc., P.O. Box 719, Uhrichsville, Ohio 44683, www.shilohrunpress.com

Our mission is to publish and distribute inspirational products offering exceptional value and biblical encouragement to the masses.

 Member of the
Evangelical Christian
Publishers Association

Printed in China.

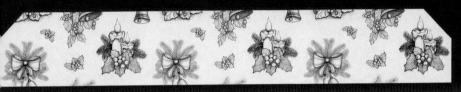

TABLE OF CONTENTS

INTRODUCTION

There is no season more wonderful, no time of year more anticipated, and no celebration more meaningful than Christmas. You love Christmas. We know that because you are reading a book about Christmas.

The signs and traditions are unmistakable: Christmas lights on every corner, Christmas music on every media channel, frantic shopping, gift giving and gift getting, church services and pageants—the list goes on.

In the midst of this flurry of activity, many of us do our best to remember the reason for Christmas. We try to stay focused on the fact that Christmas celebrates the birth of Christ. We attempt to reflect on the history, the symbols, and the spiritual meaning of Christmas that transcends the commercialism. We get that, which is why we think this book on the centuries-old tradition of Advent will help your family get ready for Christmas without being overwhelmed by it.

Advent is from the Latin word *adventus*, meaning "coming." Adventus was the Latin translation of the Greek word *parousia*, used in the New Testament to refer to the second coming of Jesus Christ. In the ancient world, before Jesus came to earth the first time, people would associate parousia with the arrival of royalty.

When you look at Advent this way, your perspective changes. No longer is Christmas just about baby Jesus being born in a stable. Advent is about preparing for the arrival of King Jesus, who came once in humility and who will come again in glory. Meanwhile, as we wait for the arrival of Jesus, Advent helps us focus on the history, the symbols, and the spiritual meaning that makes Christmas the most wonderful time of the year.

Our book has twenty-eight chapters, one for each day of the four weeks leading up to Christmas. You can read these together as a family or read them individually. Either way, we would encourage you to use the questions and suggested activities at the end of each chapter as a path to reflection. It is our prayer that the hectic pace of your family's life this Christmas will slow enough so you can see God in the small stuff of the season.

1

❧

ADVENT

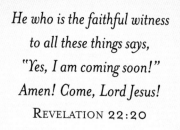

*He who is the faithful witness
to all these things says,
"Yes, I am coming soon!"
Amen! Come, Lord Jesus!*
REVELATION 22:20

One of the great joys of Christmas is the arrival of special guests. It may be a son or daughter who has been away at college or in the military. It could be a favorite aunt or uncle who has flown in for the holidays. Friends might be coming to share a holiday dinner. Whoever it is, you anticipate the arrival of your guests and prepare yourself and your home for their coming. And finally, when you hear the knock or the doorbell, you jump up, eager to welcome your loved ones into your heart and home.

That spirit and emotion are at the heart of Advent, a way of celebrating Christmas that may be new to you. Perhaps you're aware of Advent but don't know a lot about what it means or what you're supposed to do about it. When you hear the word, you probably think of candles and calendars. While those are often involved in the celebration, they are merely symbols of what Advent is all about.

The word *Advent* literally means "coming" or "arrival." When related to Christmas, it has to do with the coming of Jesus Christ. It's that period of expectant waiting and preparation for the celebration of the events surrounding the birth of Jesus.

If Advent is a new concept for you, don't feel bad. In fact, be glad that you are discovering something that can help bring the true meaning of Christmas to you and your family in a fresh way. Rather than going through the Christmas season in a frenzy, pausing for just one day to contemplate and celebrate the Savior's birth, you have the opportunity to take more time to prepare your heart and mind for the commemoration of Jesus' arrival into the world.

Traditionally, there are two ways to celebrate Advent. The first is to anticipate the coming of Christ on the four Sundays leading up to Christmas Day by lighting a candle each Sunday. Each candle represents a different aspect of the Christmas story. One tradition follows various people of the Christmas story: the prophets, Mary, the angels, and the shepherds. Another tradition emphasizes four emotions of Christmas: hope, peace, love, and joy.

Whether you follow the people or the emotions of Christmas, you celebrate Advent by lighting a candle on each of the four Sundays before Christmas—and taking time to think about what it represents. If you're doing this with your family, you can share the meaning of Christmas together and talk about why the prophets are part of the story, or why Christmas inspired hope. With either tradition, there is always a fifth candle, called a "Christ candle," that is lit on Christmas Eve or Christmas Day to signify Jesus' birth.

The second way to celebrate Advent is with an Advent calendar. There's nothing sacred about the calendar itself (just as there's nothing sacred about the candles), but like the candles, a calendar can help you think about what's sacred. The Advent calendar allows you to mark off each day of December leading up to Christmas. Typically, Advent calendars have spaces or boxes containing special images of a person, symbol, or emotion of Christmas. You can buy these calendars ready-made or make them yourself. Whichever you choose, it's a wonderful way to engage children to think about Christmas beyond the secular images of presents and Santa Claus that bombard them throughout the season.

Perhaps one of the greatest benefits of the Advent celebration—whether you use candles or a calendar or both—is that it reminds us that the coming of Christ into the world is not something that happened just once in the past. Advent tells us that Christ continues to come into our world in the present through the lives of people who choose to follow Him. And it also reminds us that Jesus is coming again in the future in the Second Advent.

Just as we delight in preparing for special guests to our physical home, we need to prepare our spiritual house for the arrival of the most special Guest of all.

❦ Don't depend on a church to celebrate Advent. Bring Advent into your home by doing one of two things (or both). First purchase an Advent candle set (you'll find them at many online stores) and light each of the candles on the four Sundays leading up to Christmas, and a fifth candle (usually white) on Christmas Eve to commemorate the birth of Jesus. Choose either the people or the emotions of Christmas and prepare a brief prayer before you light each candle so your family can experience the true meaning of Christ's coming.

❦ By doing this, you will create a sacred space in your home. In a spiritual sense, you will be preparing room for the coming of Jesus into the world.

❦ Remember, your family will never recognize the signs of Christmas until you intentionally create space in your hearts and home for Jesus.

THE STORY
OF CHRISTMAS

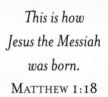

*This is how
Jesus the Messiah
was born.*

MATTHEW 1:18

Christmas is nothing if not a story. To be sure, it's more than a story (as we will see throughout this book), but it is not any less.

Most likely you and your family are well aware of the Christmas story before the start of the Advent season. Any of you could probably tell it with a great deal of accuracy without once looking in the Bible, where the Christmas story is prominently featured. You're not alone in your familiarity. For the past two thousand years, the Christmas story has captured the imagination and devotion of billions of people in every culture. There are two reasons for this.

First, as remarkable as it seems, the Christmas story is true. By definition, a story is a narrative—either true or fictitious—designed to interest or instruct the hearer or reader. There are plenty of fictitious stories that have become part of the fabric of human culture. The *Iliad* and the *Odyssey* by Homer (the ancient Greek, not the doofus dad on *The Simpsons*), and the accounts of Camelot, Robin Hood, and Santa Claus are just a few examples of legendary stories with ageless appeal—because they describe human desire and drama in universal images. But even though these stories and the characters seem larger than life, they aren't true.

In the general culture, it's likely that many people just assume that the Christmas story—with its cast of well-known characters—is a made-up tale handed down through the centuries. It's a nice story, many would say, but hardly true. After all, do you really believe in such things as angels? Or a super-bright star that moved like a guiding light across the sky, helping three wise men from the East find their way across an entire continent just to honor a baby? And then there's the part about the virgin birth. That can't be true, can it?

If you already believe the Christmas story, don't take offense if people ask such questions. They're legitimate, and it's important that we know the answers. But before we look at why the Christmas story is true, let's consider the alternative. What if the Christmas story were not true? What if it belonged on the same bookshelf as Robin Hood and Santa Claus? What difference would it make?

For one thing, the Christmas story wouldn't matter one way or the other, just like the story of Camelot doesn't matter much beyond the values of loyalty and chivalry contained in the tale. Those are important values, but you can find them in lots of stories. For another thing, if the Christmas story weren't true, it wouldn't have any power. Like the story of Santa Claus, it would fail to have much impact for anyone over the age of seven. It would be a nice story, but not one that anyone took very seriously. The fact of the matter, of course, is that the Christmas story does matter, and it is powerful.

The power of the Christmas story is the second reason why it has captured the imagination and the devotion of so many people. It tells us about God and why it was necessary for Him to reach out to His human creation in the best way possible. How was that? By sending His only Son to earth to be born of a virgin, to live a perfect life, and to make things right with God in heaven on our behalf.

Yes, the Christmas story captures our imagination year after year with its drama and color and beauty and charm. But unless we see it for what it really is—a true and powerful story that matters to every person who has ever lived—then we will never connect with the living God in a meaningful way. When we internalize its truth and personally experience the power of this story, then we are drawn into the Advent season with eager expectation to participate in the celebration of Christ's first coming to earth. And, with an eye to the future, we await the unfolding of an equally true and powerful story that has yet to unfold—the Second Coming of Christ.

. . .IN THE SEASON OF ADVENT

- All stories are meant to be told; do your best to become a Christmas storyteller. During the evenings of Advent, make it a tradition that each family member takes a turn at telling the Christmas story.

- More important than any other part of Christmas is understanding that the Christmas story is true. Take turns telling the story from a perspective of one of the characters of the story. For example, how would a shepherd tell the story? What would the story sound like if told by Mary?

- Everyone knows that the Christmas story is ancient, but let's remember that it is timeless.

- Although the story of Christmas occurred in the past, it profoundly affects your future.

- Whenever the story of God's love for humanity is explained, the story of Christmas is told.

3

GOD'S STORY

Christmas is a time when people
of all religions come together
to worship Jesus Christ.
MATT GROENING

There are so many mental pictures associated with Christmas. Whether you're in snow-covered Vermont or sweltering Palm Springs, the word *Christmas* brings to mind images of:

- a decorated tree in your family room;

- that elaborate dinner set on a festive table surrounded by family members (both the normal and the abnormal);

- traditions with the Advent wreath and lighting of the four Advent candles;

- holiday shopping;

- the anticipation of opening Christmas cards from long-ago friends;

- the stockings hung on the mantel (which are purely decorative since people stopped giving oranges as Christmas gifts); and

- brightly wrapped gifts under the tree.

Oh yes, and let's not forget the nativity scene.

For various reasons—apathy, vandalism, or political correctness—you may not see a life-size nativity in your town. But you might have a miniature version of the crèche prominently displayed in your home during the yuletide season. A little manger, holding a removable baby Jesus is always in the center; then you put Mary, seated on a hay bale, beside the manger; the kneeling Joseph is placed on the other side. Surrounding them is a wobbly stable that would probably fall over had you not strategically placed a sheep and donkey to prop it up. Also nearby are a few shepherd boys in various poses.

If you purchased the deluxe nativity kit, you also have a majestic angel with a six-inch wingspan. Since he's too heavy to place on top of the stable, you've got him taped to the wall. And the wise men, with camel, are also in the vicinity. (If you're a stickler for historical accuracy and know that the magi didn't visit Jesus until he was about two years old, you've placed the wise men, with camel, on the coffee table at the other end of the family room. That denotes their geographic distance from the manger on the night of Christ's birth.)

With the commercialization of Christmas, retailers are constantly providing a parade of paraphernalia to catch your imagination as the premier decoration for the holiday season. By its nature, the nativity scene is humble and unassuming, so it often loses out to other ornamentation with more flash and pizzazz. The status of that manger set in many homes might even be classified as a relic from Christmastimes long ago.

Although it may be modest and unpretentious, the nativity scene presents the best image of Christmas. Unlike any other ornament or decoration, the manger setting—in its singular representation—conveys the essence of Christmas: That God loved the world so much that He was willing to send His Son to earth.

As you walk past the manger display in your living room, don't be so preoccupied that you miss the significance of what it stands for. There is a great "back story" behind that collection of figurines. Don't just think of baby Jesus in a hay trough; realize that this was the Son of God who for eternity past had reigned in heaven. Imagine the celestial demotion of moving from heaven to earth, and don't overlook the indignity (and humiliation) of what He suffered when He assumed human form. (We might not consider taking on "human form" to be a cause of mortification, but it is if you are deity.)

Despite its comparatively bland appearance, the nativity scene is the premier Christmas decoration. It stands for the moment when God directly intervened into time and space to give us His Son. You don't get that kind of significance with a candy cane.

❧ Make the unveiling and placement of the nativity scene in your home a special event during Advent. A time for the family to come together and celebrate the reason for the season.

❧ Don't let God's presence be overshadowed by the Christmas presents. Place your nativity set in a place of prominence; let it be the focal point among your other decorations.

❧ Thoughts of Christmas should be more God-centered than self-centered.

❧ The decorations in your house aren't nearly as important as having the spirit of Christmas in your heart.

4

LOVE

"For this is how God loved the world:
He gave his one and only Son,
so that everyone who believes in him
will not perish but have eternal life."

JOHN 3:16

If there's one Christmas message that seems to be the most common, it's the standard, "Let there be peace on earth." Don't get us wrong: We're all for peace—on earth, in our communities, in our families, and anywhere else harmony is needed. We just happen to believe that peace isn't the central message of Christmas. True, "Peace on earth" makes for great Christmas card copy, and the angels did announce it to the shepherds on the first Christmas Eve. But there's something even more important that goes to the heart of what Christmas is all about.

In fact, we'll go so far as to say that without this "more important something," you can't have peace. Not in the world, not in your city, and for sure not in your family. You probably already know what we're talking about. It's love.

We admit that a phrase like "What the world needs now is love" doesn't sound as Christmassy as "Peace on earth." But it should, for one simple reason: Love is why we have Christmas. Don't just take our word for it. The nineteenth-century poet Christina Rossetti famously captured the spirit of love at Christmas when she wrote:

> *Love came down at Christmas,*
> *Love all lovely, love divine;*
> *Love was born at Christmas,*
> *Star and angels gave the sign.*

If that's not enough to convince you, see what the Bible says about love at Christmas:

God showed how much he loved us by sending his one
and only Son into the world so that we
might have eternal life through him.

1 JOHN 4:9

What's interesting about this demonstration of God's love is that it isn't merely a decision God made. Love is an expression of God's character, because God in His very nature is love. That's what the Bible means when it says, "God is love" (1 John 4:8). Showing how much He loves us isn't an option for God. Love is who God is, and love is what God does. The ultimate expression of God's love was His sending Jesus into the world. Like we said, love is why we have Christmas.

When we understand that God is love, we come to realize that it is in God's nature to give of Himself. He gives to bless us, though that idea flies in the face of a common belief that God is a vengeful and grumpy deity who delights in creating misery for us poor humans. Nothing could be further from the truth.

It's easy to blame God for the problems we see in the world. It's certainly easier than blaming ourselves. But that doesn't square with reality. Rather than blaming God, we need to give Him credit for providing a solution to our problems—a solution born out of love. A solution born on Christmas.

What makes love such a powerful Christmas theme is that it doesn't stop after the holiday like a truce between warring armies. Because love comes from the heart of God to us, we have the power to share that love with others. That's what the Bible means when it says, "Dear friends, since God loved us that much, we surely ought to love each other" (1 John 4:11).

The problem with peace at Christmas is that it's a two-way street. Both parties have to agree to be nice for the peace to exist. Not so with love. You don't need your unlikable neighbor or your cantankerous relative or your unreasonable boss to love you first. You can make a decision to love them preemptively with the same kind of love God shows at Christmas—and every other day of your life.

❦ Love is a difficult emotion to measure. God showed His love by sending His only Son into the world (1 John 4:9), and Jesus demonstrated His love by dying for us (Romans 5:8). Both of these expressions required an incredible sacrifice. Talk as a family about ways people can show their love for each other, not just by saying "I love you," but by showing their love.

❦ Discuss how your family can show love to others this Christmas. It may be helping another family in need or providing tangible help to a child in a third-world country. Investigate a ministry in your hometown that provides help to families and individuals in need. For global relief, we recommend World Vision.

❦ Remember, the best way to show people that God loves them is to show them love.

5

THE PROPHETS

*"All right then, the Lord himself
will give you the sign. Look!
The virgin will conceive a child!
She will give birth to a son and will
call him Immanuel (which means
'God is with us')."*

ISAIAH 7:14

Long before the month of December, we are given gentle reminders of the approaching holiday season—like the Christmas carols playing on the mall's sound system beginning the day after Halloween. Nonetheless, it seems like Christmas sneaks up on us. Even as we celebrate Advent as a time of expectant waiting and preparation for the celebration of the Savior's birth, it seems like we're never ready for it; it always comes too quickly.

The first Christmas caught people off guard as well. It came almost incognito. Oh sure, there was the star in the East, the angelic hosts, and the announcement to the shepherd boys. But nobody had marked this occasion on the calendar, and there was no pre-event publicity at the Bethlehem shopping mall. The precise date and time might have caught Mary and Joseph by surprise. (We're sure they would have preferred that the labor contractions were postponed until they had returned home to Nazareth.)

But God wasn't caught unaware by the first Christmas. It happened according to His divine plan that He put in motion centuries in advance. And He hadn't kept the plan a secret. God had given the world lots of clues about the coming birth of Jesus. Through His prophets, God proclaimed unmistakable details about the Messiah's debut:

- Approximately fourteen hundred years before Christ was born, God spoke through Moses to indicate that the Savior of the world would be born of a woman and would be a descendant of Abraham.

- The prophet Isaiah, who lived around 740 BC, clearly stated that the Messiah would be in the lineage of King David.

- Isaiah also disclosed that the Messiah would be born of a virgin. Inconceivable!

- The prophet Micah, a contemporary of Isaiah, revealed that the Messiah would be born in the sleepy town of Bethlehem.

The advance notice of the coming Messiah wasn't limited to the circumstances of that first Christmas. Bible scholars point to more than forty clear prophecies that refer to the Messiah, all of which were fulfilled by Jesus Christ alone. They include:

- That His childhood would be spent in Egypt;

- That He would ride triumphantly into Jerusalem on a donkey;

- That He would suffer for the sins of the world;

- That He would be hung on a cross, but contrary to the custom, none of His bones would be broken;

- That men would gamble for His clothes;

- His exact dying words;

- That He would come back to life after death.

Obviously, the birth of Christ was no random event. It didn't happen by accident and it was no mere coincidence. It was no fluke or twist of fate. It was part of God's intentional grand design that had been in the works since before the creation of the universe.

From time to time, you might wish that Christmas didn't arrive so quickly. You might feel frazzled because it seems that Christmas crept up on you and arrived inconveniently early. It might be that way with your family celebration on December 25. But the first Christmas came at the perfect time—precisely according to God's timetable.

...IN THE SEASON OF ADVENT

✺ While the culture around you may be spinning at warp speed during the Christmas season, let your celebration of Advent traditions be calm and tranquil. Use it as a method to slow down your family's pace so that you can take time to focus on the purpose of Advent.

✺ The prophecies of the Messiah's birth were made in such amazing detail that there was no chance of mistaken identity. Do some Bible research and make a list of these prophecies. Include the reading of these Bible verses in your Advent traditions.

✺ Sadly, the Old Testament prophets knew about the gift of the Messiah but weren't around for the celebration of His arrival. But it's worse if we, who know the true meaning of Christmas, celebrate the holiday without acknowledging the Messiah. What are some ways, other than Advent, that can be used by your family to keep a Christ-centered focus at Christmas?

6

THE COMING
MESSIAH

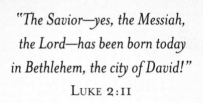

*"The Savior—yes, the Messiah,
the Lord—has been born today
in Bethlehem, the city of David!"*

LUKE 2:11

There's something about anticipation that's hard to beat. When we anticipate something—especially something really big—we tend to build it up in our mind. Sometimes, our mental build-up reaches the point that the anticipated thing, event, or person has a hard time meeting our expectations. What a letdown when that thing, event, or person doesn't quite measure up to what we had in mind.

Imagine something or someone that you once anticipated—then multiply the level of anticipation by spreading it out over a thousand years or so, with each year adding to the intensity of your expectation. Now you have some idea of what the Jews—God's chosen people—were expecting when they imagined what their "Messiah" would be like.

Throughout the Old Testament, God promised the Jews that He would deliver them from their problems by sending a king to establish God's kingdom on earth. This deliverer was referred to as "the Messiah." Moses was a great deliverer, but he never had a kingdom. In fact, no leader of Israel had a great kingdom until David came along. As the "anointed one," David was a type of *messiah* (the word literally means "anointed one"), but he was not the Messiah. Thoughtful Jews understood that no human king could fulfill the high ideal of the Messiah, who would be God coming down to earth.

After David's great earthly kingdom came to an end, the prophets of Israel began endowing the anticipated Messiah with names that clearly placed Him beyond mere mortals. He would be "Wonderful Counselor, Mighty God, Everlasting Father, Prince of Peace" (Isaiah 9:6). Furthermore, the Messiah would be:

- 🌾 A direct descendant of King David (Isaiah 11:1);

- 🌾 Born in Bethlehem, David's own birthplace (Micah 5:2); and

- 🌾 Born of a virgin (Isaiah 7:14).

So the stage was set, and the time was right for God to send the great Deliverer to rescue His people—and that's what God did. He sent Jesus, the Messiah, the Anointed One, who was a descendant of David (Luke 1:31–33), born in Bethlehem, (Luke 2:4, 6–7) and born of a virgin (Matthew 1:18, 22–23). God even sent one of His personal messengers, an angel who proclaimed on that first Christmas Eve:

"I bring you good news that will bring great joy to all people. The Savior—yes, the Messiah, the Lord—has been born today in Bethlehem, the city of David! And you will recognize him by this sign: You will find a baby wrapped snugly in strips of cloth, lying in a manger."

LUKE 2:10–12

There was no mistaking it. The prophecies had been fulfilled. God had come to earth in the person of Jesus. The Messiah had come. Surely the Jews would embrace their king.

There was only one problem. They were anticipating a different kind of Messiah, and the baby lying in the manger didn't measure up to their ideal. They expected a royal king born in a palace; what God sent them was a common baby born in a stable. They expected a birth announcement to be made to the religious leaders; God first told a bunch of lowly shepherds. They anticipated a conquering king who would deal with their enemies and rule politically; Jesus came to serve and to give His life for others.

It's easy to criticize the Jews for missing the real point and rejecting Jesus the Messiah. But before we do that, we need to look at ourselves and ask what kind of Deliverer we're looking for. Are we expecting Jesus to deliver us from our problems? Are we expecting Jesus to deliver us from our enemies? Are we expecting Jesus to deliver us from poverty and sickness? Jesus can do all of those things, but that's not why He came. More than anything else, Jesus the Messiah came to deliver us from our sins.

❧ Some of the most amazing prophecies in the Bible concern the coming Messiah. We have already listed a few of them. Here are a few others to review with your family. We have provided the Old Testament reference where the prophecy originated, along with the New Testament reference showing that the prophecy was fulfilled.

- Although born in Bethlehem, He would spend His childhood in Egypt (Hosea 11:1; Matthew 2:13–15).
- He would have a ceremonial entrance into Jerusalem on a donkey (Zechariah 9:9; Matthew 21:2, 4, 5).
- He would be put to death so that we could be saved (Isaiah 53:5; Matthew 27:32–35).
- He would come back to life after His death (Psalm 10:9,10; John 20:1-10).

❧ The true Messiah doesn't simply meet the expectations of those looking for deliverance. He exceeds them.

7

THE NAMES
OF JESUS

An angel of the Lord appeared to him in a dream. "Joseph, son of David," the angel said, "do not be afraid to take Mary as your wife. For the child within her was conceived by the Holy Spirit. And she will have a son, and you are to name him Jesus."

MATTHEW 1:20–21

Selecting a name for a newborn child can be difficult. Most expectant parents spend many months writing lists of "boy names" and "girl names." Maybe that's why God designed the human gestation period to be nine months in duration. It usually takes that long for the mother and father to agree on mutually acceptable monikers. A lot of factors must be considered:

- ❧ How does it sound with the last name? (You can't name a baby girl "Sandy" if her last name is "Beach.")

- ❧ Did either the mother or the father date a person with this name while in high school?

- ❧ Will the bullies on the playground find the name too easy to rhyme? (Take "Meyer" off the "boy's name" list, because you don't want him called "Meyer the Cryer." Oh, children can be so cruel.)

- ❧ Is the name too archaic (like "Winifred")? Or, is it a name that simply suggests that the parents were trying too hard to be different (like "Xerox")?

Besides the phonetic sound of the baby's potential name, parents often consider the derivation and meaning behind the name. This factor is mainly promoted by the publishers of those "baby name" books. In our twenty-first century Western culture, there isn't much meaning associated with specific names. No parent really thinks about name derivations when they are yelling for "Tyler" or "Jorun" to come downstairs for dinner.

Mary and Joseph probably didn't make a list of name ideas for their baby. It isn't that they were cavalier about naming their child. Quite the contrary. The meaning of a name was a really big deal in first-century Middle Eastern culture; every utterance of that name—throughout the child's life—was closely associated with its historical meaning and considered a source of power. But Mary and Joseph could focus their mental energies on the other concerns that panic expectant parents. The name of their child had been preselected by God.

In separate dreams, an angel had appeared to Joseph and to Mary. The angel declared that Mary would give birth to a baby boy whose name would be "Jesus." (This was another clue to Mary and Joseph that this would be no ordinary child because Jesus means "the Lord saves.")

And baby Jesus didn't lack for nicknames either. About four hundred years earlier, the prophet Isaiah had declared that the child born to be the Messiah would also be known by four other distinctly royal titles. Consider what these names reveal about the kind of man the baby Jesus would become:

 Wonderful Counselor—Wonderful typically referred to supernatural, so the Messiah was one who was characterized by perfect wisdom.

🌿 *Mighty God*—This is a term that predicted the Messiah's ultimate triumph over evil.

🌿 *Everlasting Father*—The Messiah is a protective Father who guards His children for all eternity.

🌿 *Prince of Peace*—He brings peace in the complete sense of wholeness and reconciliation with God for every individual.

Of course, when Jesus was born, Mary and Joseph didn't look at Him in His swaddling clothes and say, "Isn't He the cutest little Everlasting Father you have ever seen." And when Jesus was playing stickball in the streets of Nazareth as an eleven-year-old kid, nobody said, "Wow, that Wonderful Counselor can really swing the bat." And as a kid, He was probably never accused of having a Messiah complex (although those accusations were made about twenty years later). He was just plain ol' Jesus, the son of Joseph the carpenter.

But almost two thousand years later, we have the advantage of looking at His life from a retrospective vantage point. While He was just "Jesus" at birth, we have the privilege of reading the historical record of His life and resurrection. We can see that He lived up to the names that were bestowed upon Him. Think about that the next time you hear the lyrics to "Away in a Manger." That wasn't just the baby Jesus in the manger; it was the Savior of the world. And He had the names to prove it.

❦ There is no name as universally recognized as "Jesus." But use your Advent celebration time to refer to Him by His other titles. On different days, focus on a different title and discuss its meanings. What does each title teach us about Him?

❦ If Mary and Joseph had been allowed to name their child, it might have been baby Joseph, Jr., lying in the manger. Of the multiple names given in the Bible for Jesus, which one is most meaningful to you?

❦ Most children are told to live up to their family name. Jesus was deserving of His royal titles at the moment of His birth.

❦ To His parents, He was known as Jesus, but you can know Him as "Savior." And we can also describe Him by His character traits. He shares the same attributes as the Holy Spirit, whose qualities are found in Galatians 5:22–23. Read these verses and discuss ways in which Jesus displayed these characteristics in His life.

8

HOPE

*Faith is the confidence that what
we hope for will actually happen;
it gives us assurance about
things we cannot see.*

HEBREWS 11:1

Christmas is a season of hope and wonder:

- Most kids have a particular gift they hope for, and they wonder if they are going to get it.

- A wife has the hope that her husband will get her a romantic gift, but she realistically wonders what electrical appliance she'll receive from him.

- We all hope not to get another fruitcake from the relatives, and when it arrives, we wonder if they will recognize it later in the backyard garden as a decorative boulder.

In these contexts, hope is merely a form of wishing. But the true spirit of hope at Christmastime has a much deeper and richer meaning. The hope of Christmas denotes an expectation with certainty. Christmas hope is a confident assurance that something will happen. It is a hope that you can hang on to when the rest of life seems shaky.

Christmas hope is thousands of years old, rooted in the history of the Jews. God had promised them a Messiah who would be their deliverer. They relied on this hope when they were enslaved by Pharaoh in Egypt (about 1700 BC). The promise of the Messiah also sustained them during the invasion of Israel when many of them were taken captive and transported to Assyria (about 700 BC) and when Jerusalem was destroyed and the Jews were exiled to Babylon (about 600 BC). And, during the earthly lifetime of Jesus, with the Jews suffering under the tyranny of the Roman government, they anxiously waited for the Messiah to lead a political revolt.

The birth of Christ—what we celebrate as Christmas—was the fulfillment of God's promise to send a Messiah. But few people recognized it as that. Their oversight is understandable. They were expecting the arrival of a conquering hero. They didn't imagine that their Deliverer would come dressed in a diaper. They wanted to see Him standing tall, holding a sword in His outstretched hand. They weren't expecting an infant squirming in a hay-strewn feeding trough.

Even when He grew to be a man, few people recognized Jesus as the Messiah. The people wanted relief from Roman oppression, but Christ told them how to be free from sin and guilt. They wanted financial prosperity, but Christ spoke of success in terms of being reconciled with God. They wanted political peace, but Jesus offered spiritual peace. He wasn't what they were looking for—but the fact remains that God delivered on His promise to send what they needed, whether they realized it or not.

Now, about two thousand years later, God is still in the promise-keeping business. The Bible contains promises that God has made and not forgotten:

✾   You can turn to Him in times of crisis;

✾   He will provide for you in times of need; and

✾   He loves you as His own child.

Skeptics might say that these are empty promises—nothing more than wishful thinking. But the hope of Christmas proves the skeptics wrong. These are the promises of the same God who made good on His pledge to send a Messiah. The God who invaded earth with His presence on that first Christmas night to fulfill His promise is the same God who can fulfill His promises to you.

God has proven Himself to be reliable. He can be trusted. Though the difficulties of life might make you question God's faithfulness, He is a worthy recipient of your hope. Maybe that is one reason He's given us the hope of Christmas. It is a perennial reminder that God keeps His promises. And you can hang your hope on that.

❦ The Bible says, "Hope deferred makes the heart sick, but a longing fulfilled is a tree of life" (Proverbs 13:12 NIV). Ask each family member to remember a time when the things they hoped for didn't happen, or a Christmas in the past when they didn't get the present they wanted. How did they feel? (Encourage complete honesty!) Now have everyone share how it felt to get something they hoped for.

❦ Discuss how God knows what we want, but He also knows what we need. Talk about the difference between "wants" and "needs," especially during the season of Advent.

❦ Ask everyone to answer this question: Who knows better what we need, God or us? Why?

❦ The hope of Christmas is the confident assurance that God is in control and knows what He's doing.

9

THE ANCESTRY
OF JESUS

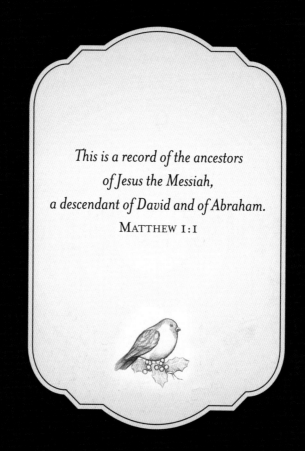

*This is a record of the ancestors
of Jesus the Messiah,
a descendant of David and of Abraham.*

MATTHEW 1:1

Have you ever wondered what your ancestors were like? Maybe you've studied your family tree to get a portrait of your heritage. It can be a revealing exercise, because your past can shed a lot of light on your present.

Most people who follow Jesus know a fair amount about His life on earth—His miracles, His teachings, His death and resurrection. But they know very little about His past. That's probably because few people think Jesus had a past, at least a past on earth. Most people, if they've given the topic any thought at all, probably believe the life of Jesus on earth started when He came down from heaven to be born in Bethlehem and concluded about thirty-three years later when He returned to heaven.

It would be easy to conclude this if all we had were the Gospels of Mark and John. These two biographies of Jesus start with Jesus as an adult. But those are just two of the four books about the life of Christ in the New Testament. If you read Matthew and Luke, not only do you find a description of the birth of Christ, but a record of His ancestry as well.

In fact, Matthew starts with the ancestry of Jesus, telling us right off the bat that Jesus was a descendant of both David and Abraham. This detail is significant because God made promises to each man: That one of Abraham's descendants would bless the whole world (Genesis 12:2–3) and one of David's would establish an eternal kingdom (2 Samuel 7:12–13). In both cases that person turned out to be Jesus.

In Matthew's genealogy, Jesus is presented as the legal male descendant of David, through adoption by Joseph, making Him heir to King David's eternal throne. To anyone seeking a legal qualification for Jesus as Messiah, this list of ancestors is all they need.

But Matthew doesn't stop there. While he's careful to present Jesus as the ultimate and perfect fulfillment of the promise God made to David (that His kingdom would go on forever), Matthew also shows that the ancestors of Jesus were very human. True, the cast of characters (which spans two thousand years) includes some heroes of the faith, such as Abraham, Isaac, and David. But most of the ancestors in the human bloodline of Jesus were quite ordinary, and some— Rahab and Tamar stand out—had less than sterling reputations. Others were downright nasty. In other words, the ancestry of Jesus isn't all that different than yours or ours.

Why was Jesus, the Son of God, born into such a "human" family? Because Jesus came to earth to save all people: kings and heroes, ordinary people and scoundrels, honest people and thieves. When we look at the ancestry of Jesus—something we tend to skip over in order to get to the story of Jesus' life—we can see that His past impacts our present and our future.

For all of us living two millennia after the birth of Jesus, His ancestry assures us that God has always worked through all kinds of people to accomplish His purposes. It also tells us that He can work through us now, regardless of where we came from or where we fit on the family tree.

As you continue to anticipate the coming of Jesus in this season of Advent, remember that Jesus came in the past as the descendent of real people—some quite ordinary and others rather extraordinary. And He did it so He could fully embody our humanity without sacrificing any of His divinity.

❦ Talk as a family about your ancestry. If you are unclear about your great- and great-great grandparents, you could do some research (the Internet has plenty of sites to help you). But be prepared! There might be some surprises along the way. That's okay. God made us to be in a family and to stay connected with our family, no matter when they lived or who they are.

❦ Thank God together for the sacrifices made by your ancestors so you could live where you live and enjoy the privileges you have.

❦ Pray for those children and grandchildren who will follow you. The prayers of God's children for God's children are more effective than you could ever imagine.

❦ The divinity of Jesus means He can save us. The humanity of Jesus means He understands us.

10

MARY

"Don't be afraid, Mary," the angel told her, "for you have found favor with God! You will conceive and give birth to a son, and you will name him Jesus. He will be very great and will be called the Son of the Most High..." And he will reign over Israel forever; his Kingdom will never end!"

LUKE 1: 30–33

Mary has been praised throughout history, but her own generation wasn't too kind to her. Imagine the scandal. A young woman (possibly sixteen years of age) who became pregnant outside of marriage. In that time and in that culture, her situation was disastrous. Try to imagine the pressure and stress that Mary endured—not to mention the sarcastic comments.

- First of all, who would believe her alibi? An angel appeared to her. (Yeah, right. How convenient that the angel came alone to her at night, so nobody else could confirm the sighting.)

- And the theological aspects of her story seemed preposterous: She is going to give birth to the Messiah? (Sure. God is selecting a young, obscure girl out of poverty from the hick town of Nazareth to be the birth mother of divine royalty.)

- The physiological side of her story was equally incredible: She became pregnant because the "Holy Spirit came upon her." (An immaculate conception! This story is inconceivable! If she's actually pregnant, then she's a tramp. But if it turns out that she isn't pregnant, maybe she's just insane.)

But the gossip mill in her hometown of Nazareth wasn't the worst part. She had to tell Joseph that she was pregnant, and he knew that he wasn't the father. Imagine the suspense as she waited for his reaction. Would he call off their engagement? If he abandoned her, she would certainly be a social reject the rest of her life; no one would marry her. Mary's only recourse would be to turn to her own father, but even he might cast her out of his household in disgrace. She had seen women in this plight living on the outskirts of town, and they had only two career choices: prostitution or begging.

When viewed in this light, being "favored" by God doesn't seem so special, does it? But perhaps that's the lesson God is trying to teach us through the life story of Mary. God's blessings don't exactly translate into a life of fame and fortune, peace and prosperity. To the contrary, from the time she was confronted by the angel Gabriel, she probably encountered more pain than pleasure.

- At the outset, there was the scandal of her out-of-wedlock pregnancy.

- Then there came the difficult circumstances of using a stable as a delivery room.

- Then, when King Herod issued a decree to kill all Jewish baby boys, Mary and Joseph packed up the baby Jesus and became fugitives, escaping to Egypt.

❦ As her son grew into manhood, Mary lived with the constant reminder that the ancient prophet Isaiah had predicted that the Messiah would be tortured. She knew her son was the One the prophets referred to as the "suffering servant." She lived with the unabating, penetrating pain of knowing that her son would be slaughtered for the sins of the world.

❦ And she was an eyewitness to His torment and crucifixion.

Yet Mary didn't hesitate to accept God's plan for her life. There is no indication that she ever complained or cursed God for the circumstances she endured as part of His plan. Quite the contrary. Her response to Gabriel was a resounding, "'I am the Lord's servant. May everything you have said about me come true'" (Luke 1:38).

At Christmastime it's customary for people to gather in prayer and thank the Lord for His favor and many blessings. But the story of Mary suggests that His favor may involve putting us through difficult circumstances in order to accomplish His plans. Are we truly willing servants, ready to accept whatever He wants? Maybe it takes that attitude to realize that we are blessed with God's favor simply by His love for us.

❧ Try to imagine yourself being in Mary's circumstances. Think of different stages and events in her life. Describe what she might have been feeling.

❧ When Mary learned that Christ had risen from the tomb, do you think she might have considered that the hardships during her life were all part of God's perfect plan?

❧ What about you? Describe a difficult circumstance that you are presently enduring. Can you take an eternal perspective to find God's blessings in your present situation?

❧ The essence of God's grace is His favor. Mary had God's favor, and so do you.

❧ You'll miss out on many of God's blessings if you don't expect to find them in the midst of difficulties.

11

GLORY

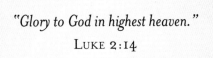

"Glory to God in highest heaven."

LUKE 2:14

If you were to make a list of your favorite things about Christmas, would you include glory? You'd probably have things like joy, peace, love, gifts, miracles, and lights in your top ten. (Hopefully, you would not include whiskers on kittens and warm woolen mittens.) But would glory be in the mix?

We certainly would not have included it in our list, but that was before we did a little research. We found that glory characterizes the spirit of Christmas as much as any other word, but it probably is one of the best Christmas words out there.

For one thing, you find glory throughout the biblical account of what happened at Christmas. Mary gave God glory in response to the news that she would bear the Savior of the world (Luke 1:46). When the angels announced to the shepherds that Jesus had been born, they sang out, "'Glory to God in highest heaven'" (Luke 2:14). And when the apostle John wrote about Jesus, he said, "And we have seen his glory, the glory of the Father's one and only Son" (John 1:14).

Truth is, glory is all over the Christmas story. So why don't we talk more about it? We suspect it has something to do with the word itself. We're uncomfortable with people who seek glory. An athlete who draws attention to himself is sometimes called a "glory hound." Someone assigned to a project who takes all the credit is said to "want all the glory." The bottom line is that we don't like people who like glory.

But that's because we're talking about people. The kind of

glory referred to in the Bible, especially in the Christmas story, is glory directed to God. And that's an entirely different matter. Human glory is usually related to performance, but God's glory has to do with His person. The reason scripture tells us to give God glory is not because He needs it to feed His ego—it's because God by definition is glorious and worthy of all the glory we can give Him. When applied to God, *glory* simply means "honor" or "excellence." Even more, it implies that God's character is perfect (Romans 3:23).

Because God is Spirit, we can't see Him. But we can see the created brightness that surrounds God as He reveals Himself to us. For one thing, God reveals Himself through His creation: A brilliant sunset, a flash of lightning, and the canopy of stars above are nature's way of giving God glory (Psalm 104:2). In another more specific and even more powerful way, the invisible God has revealed Himself through the visible person of Jesus Christ, who is the light of the world (John 8:12).

This is why glory belongs in the Christmas story. The Bible says God became a human in the form of Jesus, also called the Living Word, in order to show His glory to the world:

So the Word became human and made his home among us.
He was full of unfailing love and faithfulness. And we have seen
his glory, the glory of the Father's one and only Son.

JOHN 1:14

Just what does all this glory mean to us? How does it impact our lives, especially in the everyday small stuff of life? Quite simply, God created us so we could reflect God's glory. To put it another way, God made us to make Him look good. Even as the beauty of nature makes its Creator look good, our purpose is to make God look good by doing those things He wants us to do, especially during this Advent season of glory.

❧ Here's an Advent activity for each member of your family: Give each person a piece of paper so they can make a list of those things God has done for them this year that should motivate them to praise Him and give Him glory. (If there are little ones in your family, make the list for them.) Now share these with one another. You may be surprised at what you learn, and it will definitely encourage you to give God glory.

❧ Now have everyone turn their paper over and list at least one thing they have done lately to bring glory to God.

❧ Giving glory to God in the highest means just that—giving God the highest place in our lives.

❧ Because Jesus reveals God's glory to the world, He is the world's true light.

12

❧

JOSEPH

Joseph, Mary's fiancé, was a good man
and did not want to disgrace her publicly,
so he decided to break the engagement
quietly. As he considered this, an angel
of the Lord appeared to him in a dream.
"Joseph, son of David," the angel said,
"do not be afraid to take
Mary as your wife."
MATTHEW 1:19–20

Joseph was just an ordinary guy who—in God's design—got caught up in the most extraordinary events in human history. He wasn't seeking notoriety or a place in history. He was just a regular Joe (pun intended) who wouldn't have suspected that he had the qualifications to be the stepfather of the Son of God.

Joseph wasn't super-spiritual. He certainly lacked the credentials of Zechariah, who held a prominent position as priest in the temple in Jerusalem. The Bible describes Zechariah and his wife, Elizabeth, as "righteous in God's eyes" (Luke 1:6). That's a pretty good endorsement etched in the pages of scripture. It doesn't mean they were perfect, but it does imply that they were sincere in their love of God, and that their obedience to God was motivated out of love for Him.

It doesn't appear that Joseph had this kind of reputation in his community. He most likely was a God-fearing man who tried with relative success to be obedient to God. (It's doubtful that Mary's father would have sanctioned the engagement to his daughter if Joseph had been a religious slacker.) Maybe Joseph volunteered for janitorial duty at his synagogue on Thursday nights—but it's likely that no one would have called him a spiritual pillar of the community.

Joseph wasn't particularly successful, and certainly not prosperous. He was a tradesman in a rural town. His town of Nazareth was little more than a pit stop on a trade route between much better places. Its roads were dusty, and its people were crusty. It wasn't held in high regard. So Joseph was a nobody in a nowhere town. In a culture that had clearly-defined socioeconomic separations, Joseph became engaged to a young girl from a poor family. That tells us that his net worth was pretty paltry. If there was a flourishing business in Nazareth, it wasn't Joseph's carpentry shop.

Other than his lineage and his residency, the Bible gives only one other background clue about this Joseph: He was a just man. That tells us he was fair and attempted to do the right thing. His gesture to quietly release the pregnant Mary from their engagement contract—rather than following the tradition of putting her through a public humiliation—is evidence of his honor. This is an admirable virtue, but it makes for a short résumé if you're applying to adopt the baby Messiah.

But in God's paradigm, credentials, qualifications, and past accomplishments are basically irrelevant. God is more interested in your attitude about serving Him. And in this category, Joseph was stellar. The Bible captures the essence of Joseph's heart for God with this single sentence: "When Joseph woke up, he did as the angel of the Lord commanded" (Matthew 1:24).

That's what God is looking for. Ordinary people who simply obey when God calls them. Joseph was not asked to assume an easy assignment. But he didn't try to dodge the work by pleading unworthiness or incompetence. He didn't protest or try to negotiate the terms of the task. He didn't suggest the names of others who could do a better job. He simply responded in the manner that God had requested.

God hasn't changed His tactics in the last two thousand years. He's still looking for ordinary people to be part of His extraordinary plan. He isn't recruiting the best-qualified and most successful candidates. He specializes in using obscure people with obedient hearts. He wants to use people who—like Joseph—will wake up and do what He commands.

When Joseph woke up after his dream, he took a mighty leap outside his comfort zone. He could not imagine the consequences that would follow his obedience. But that didn't stop him. He didn't delay his response to take an inventory of all of his emotional feelings and gut reactions. He simply acted in obedience to God's call. Now that is something to put on a résumé.

❧ Here's a role-playing activity for Advent: Suppose that you are a parent, and your daughter announces that she wants to marry Joseph. If you wanted to discourage the marriage, what arguments would you make to your daughter about Joseph's undesirable prospects?

❧ Now, suppose that your daughter was influenced by your arguments, but was praying for guidance from God. What words might God say to your daughter to endorse Joseph as a good candidate for marriage?

❧ We should be more concerned about hearing God's call than the consequence that may befall.

❧ If you think that you are worthy to serve God, your ego disqualifies you from doing so.

❧ When you know you are incapable without God, then there is little argument about who should get the credit for the accomplishment.

13

FAITH

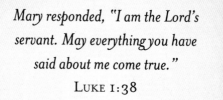

Mary responded, "I am the Lord's servant. May everything you have said about me come true."

LUKE 1:38

If you would argue that the Christmas story requires a lot of faith, we would agree—but not for the reason you might think. If by "faith" you mean "blind faith"—because there's just no way to know for sure that the events on that first Christmas happened the way the Bible says they did—that's not what we mean. It doesn't take any more faith to believe the historic fact that Jesus was born than it does to believe the historic fact that George Washington crossed the Delaware River. In both cases we have reliable information based on trustworthy witnesses, giving us good reason to believe these events happened—even though we weren't there to see them ourselves.

On the other hand, if by "faith" you refer to the action required on our part to respond to what we believe to be true, then we are on the same page.

You see, it's one thing to believe that Jesus was born on Christmas Day and quite another matter to live your life as if this were actually true. By way of example, think about an airplane. You can have faith that a certain airplane will fly, but until you actually get on board and demonstrate your confidence in the plane, your faith doesn't count for much. It isn't an active, living faith.

Now think about Christmas. Rather than simply believing the Christmas story is true, insert yourself into the story. Think what it would have been like to believe the events would actually happen—before they happened. Imagine yourself as Joseph or Mary, both of whom were asked by God's messenger to do something extraordinary and quite unbelievable: To have faith in God that His only Son—the Savior who was coming to take away the sins of the world—was going to be born through them. Keep in mind that this was before anything had happened. They were asked to trust God before there was any physical evidence.

What if Mary and Joseph had believed God without acting on their belief? What if they had not accepted the assignment God gave them? Because we know that God will always carry out His plans, it is certain He would have found two other people to get the job done.

Real faith—the kind that is so evident in the Christmas story—is more than knowledge about something. Real faith is about personally trusting God and believing that what He says is true, even before it happens. When we have that kind of faith, we have no choice but to respond to God's call on our lives the way Mary did:

> *"I am the Lord's servant. May everything you have said about me come true."*
> LUKE 1:38

What is our faith worth if we don't trust God completely? When faced with a challenge or an opportunity to get on board with God, our natural tendency is to trust our own abilities and our own understanding of the situation. We don't want to act unless we're absolutely certain we can get the job done. But God will never use us if we take that approach. He wants us to trust Him with all our heart. He doesn't want us to depend on ourselves, but to seek His will in all we do.

If we do that, like Mary and Joseph and so many other great heroes of the faith have, God promises to direct us in all we do—in the small stuff as well as the big—as He uses our work and our words for His glory.

❋ Read about Joseph in Matthew 1:18–25. Have one family member take on the role of Joseph and answer these questions:

- Why did Joseph want to separate himself from Mary?
- Did he have a legitimate reason to do this?
- What did the angel say that convinced Joseph to follow through and marry Mary?

❋ Now have another family member read about Mary in Luke 1:26–38 and answer these questions:

- After Gabriel appeared and spoke to Mary, what was her primary concern?
- What was the angel's explanation, and how did Mary respond?

❋ What can your family learn from the way Joseph and Mary accepted their assignments?

❋ When you have faith, you have confident assurance that what you hope for and what God promises are going to happen.

14

BETHLEHEM

But you, O Bethlehem. . .are only a small
village among all the people of Judah.
Yet a ruler of Israel, whose origins are in
the distant past, will come from you. . . .
And he will stand to lead his flock with
the LORD's strength, in the majesty
of the name of the LORD his God.

MICAH 5:2, 4

What was God thinking? The event of the Messiah's birth was the perfect public relations opportunity. This was the celebrity birth of all eternity, and God could have caused media frenzy had He staged it differently. So why choose a tiny podunk town like Bethlehem for the big event?

If God had wanted worldwide attention for His Son's birth, He could have picked the then center of the known universe, Rome. It was the cultural, political, and commercial nucleus of the first-century world. If the Messiah's birth had happened in Rome, the news could have been quickly disseminated around the globe.

But even if God wanted to put a Jewish spin on the Messiah's birth, He could have arranged for it to take place in Jerusalem. In the religious realm, Jerusalem had been the Holy City throughout Hebrew history. While Jerusalem didn't have the cultural cache of Rome, it was a credible metropolis in its own right and certainly a worthy site for the birth of God's Son.

An argument could even be made for Jesus to be born in Nazareth, the residence of both Joseph and Mary. This would make sense, as Mary could have given birth with the aid of her mother and other relatives. East or west, home is best.

But Bethlehem? Why Bethlehem? It was a sleepy little village populated by sheepherders and farmers. Although it was only five miles south of Jerusalem, the two cities were worlds apart. There was nothing distinctive or special about it. Its only claim to fame was that it was the hometown of a young boy who killed a giant and then went on to assume the throne for all of Israel. But that had been about a thousand years ago. So village leaders were grasping at ancient history when they inscribed "Home of King David" on the WELCOME TO BETHLEHEM signs.

The answer to this quandary can be found in the writing of the ancient prophet Micah. About seven hundred years before the birth of Christ, God spoke through the prophet to declare that the Messiah would be born in the town of Bethlehem. This was a specific prophecy that could be fact-checked against anyone claiming to be the Messiah.

God frequently does things in ways that seem strange at the time. Often, His wisdom is revealed only when viewed after the fact. And so it is with the selection of Bethlehem as the Messiah's birthplace. Arranging for Jesus to be born in Rome or Jerusalem or even Nazareth would make sense to human understanding. But God wanted to prove that He was involved in every detail of this event.

Contemporary historians and statisticians can confirm it would have taken a miracle to have Mary's child born in Bethlehem when she and Joseph lived seventy miles to the north. Why would they venture on such a dangerous sojourn to Bethlehem, putting both Mary and the unborn child at great risk, when it was less a desirable place than Nazareth?

God knew all along that the Roman emperor, Caesar Augustus, would order everyone to travel to the hometown of their ancestors to register for a census. Since both Joseph and Mary were in the lineage of King David, they were required to travel to Bethlehem at the precise time Mary was expected to deliver her child. A coincidence? Hardly, if God knew the timing and had Micah announce the unlikely birth site hundreds of years in advance.

Can anyone really believe that Jesus was born in Bethlehem by happenstance or accident? No, and that is precisely why God orchestrated the circumstances in this fashion.

God works in the same way in your life. Just as He was intimately involved in the design details for the first Christmas, He is working in your life today.

❦ Spend some time on the Internet, finding information and pictures of Bethlehem. In particular, look for pictures which reflect the scenery and the buildings as they might have looked at the time when Jesus was born. Does this place look to you to be a place suitable for the arrival of a King? What you find may appear to be a God-forsaken place. But in fact, it was God-blessed.

❦ Bethlehem rose out of obscurity when its population increased by One.

❦ The beauty of a miracle in your life is not primarily what it does for you but the attention that it brings to God.

15

THE INN AND
THE STABLE

She gave birth to her first child, a son.
She wrapped him snugly in strips of
cloth and laid him in a manger,
because there was no lodging
available for them.

LUKE 2:7

One of the most reviled characters in the Bible is the innkeeper who rejected Mary and Joseph on the night Jesus was born. The young couple had journeyed from Nazareth to Bethlehem and was badly in need of a room for the night. Not only did they need shelter, they needed a warm and clean place for the "obviously pregnant" Mary to give birth. Unfortunately, the man who ran the village inn—often portrayed as a crude, heartless fellow—refused to provide a room, forcing a desperate Joseph to seek refuge for his wife and soon-to-be-born son in a stable full of animals.

Whenever this story is told, many develop a hatred for the innkeeper—putting him just one notch above Judas Iscariot, the renegade disciple who would betray Jesus thirty-three years later. To be sure, the story of the innkeeper makes for good drama. There's only one problem. This much-maligned fellow is never mentioned in the Bible. There's not even any evidence that such a character ever existed.

The other elements of this well-known story are true, although the Bible is light on the details of the full-to-capacity inn and the stable where Jesus was born. Yes, there was a village lodging place, but contrary to the embellished images you will often see in picture books, it probably wasn't a hotel with rooms, like some ancient Holiday Inn. More likely, as was the custom, it was a guest room in a private residence, or it could have been some sort of public shelter. Given Bethlehem's crowded conditions at the time of the census, it's not surprising that there were no rooms available that holy night. The only space for the young couple was a place reserved for animals.

Interestingly, the Bible never mentions animals either. All it says is that Mary gave birth to a son, wrapped Him in strips of cloth (it was a sign of motherly care and affection to "swaddle" her baby in such a manner), and laid Him in a manger. The Bible doesn't tell us if sheep were bleating or cattle were lowing. It just says Mary put Jesus in a manger. However, since a manger was a feeding trough for animals, we can safely infer that Jesus was born with animals around.

As for the stable itself, it probably wasn't a quaint little barn like the ones you see in the picture books. In those days in Palestine, animals were often kept in a lower level room or stall attached to the living quarters of a private residence. Or it could have been a cave used as a shelter for animals, another common practice in that time.

Whatever the nature of the stable, it was a place suitable for animals, not the Savior of the world. Still, given the prophecies about the Messiah—"He was despised and rejected. . . . We turned our backs on him and looked the other way. He was despised, and we did not care" (Isaiah 53:3)—the setting of His birth was entirely appropriate. This humble beginning in a dark and dirty stable shows us the humility of Jesus, and it foreshadows the fact that He would attain glory through suffering.

Maybe the Jews expected their Messiah to be born in royal splendor, but this was never God's plan. This was never what Jesus had in mind.

Though he was God, he did not think of equality with God as something to cling to. Instead, he gave up his divine privileges; he took the humble position of a slave and was born as a human being.
PHILIPPIANS 2:6–7

We should never limit God by our own expectations. He is at work wherever He's needed in our dark and dirty world, and He's looking for those who would willingly and faithfully follow Him.

What about the innkeeper—whether he actually existed or not? Rather than despise him we should use him as an example, a reminder to always have room for the Savior in our hearts and in our lives, whether it's during the season of Advent or any other time of year.

❀ You may have a small "manger set"—sometimes called a nativity set or crèche—as part of the Christmas decorations you set up during the season. As a family, take a look at each piece and describe what it must have been like to be one of the people in the set—Mary, Joseph, the angel, shepherds, wise men, even baby Jesus. (If you don't have a crèche, find a representation through a Google search.)

❀ If you have some animals in your crèche, imagine what they would have sounded like (or smelled like). How did their presence add to or detract from the miraculous scene before them?

❀ God delights in using humble things—and humble people—to carry out His plans. Think about how God can use you during this Advent season.

16

THE BIRTH
OF JESUS

I dreamed it was Christmas Eve, and while waiting for a green light I noticed the manger scene on the church lawn. It's all so overwhelming, this Christmas business, *I thought. The shopping and singing and partying and gift wrapping and Santa Claus and Jesus. I feel wonderful then guilty then joyful then confused.* God help me, *I thought. And the light changed, and the baby in the manger smiled.*

JOE HICKMAN

Our mental pictures of the night of Christ's birth are probably unrealistic. Most likely, we're guilty of imagining the event as much more pristine than it really was. With the stained glass images of the manger scene, and the little halo above the baby Jesus' head in those Renaissance paintings, we know that the Son of God was there in the stable. But we tend to picture Him as God in a pint-sized human package. We forget that baby Jesus was equally human, with all the complications that accompany birth.

To fully understand the fact that Jesus was both God and man, we need to accurately envision what happened in the stable that first Christmas night. Maybe the events began earlier in the afternoon with Mary doubled over in pain, her contractions increasing in frequency. There was no place for her to lie down, because she and Joseph were still on the hunt for lodging. She couldn't ride comfortably on the donkey, and she couldn't walk without severe distress. She was miserable.

Joseph wasn't in pain, but he was probably panicked. He was doing a poor job of providing and protecting when Mary most needed his help. Perhaps he was frantic to find a safe place for her, fearing that she might injure herself or the baby if she wasn't soon settled.

As afternoon became evening, Mary's contractions grew relentless, her cries of pain perhaps so loud that she could have been heard by the shepherds outside of town—if they hadn't been distracted by the singing of the angelic hosts. Joseph, who had probably only been involved in his own birth, was useless as a midwife. All he could manage to do was to wipe the sweat from Mary's forehead and pray that this baby would make a quick entrance.

Our antiseptic view of the birth of Christ would be shattered if we had seen the real event. It was messy and unsanitary. The hay was soaked in blood. The animals were probably frightened by Mary's cries, jumping about and kicking up dust. In the midst of this chaos, the baby Jesus was born, not at all plump and adorable. He was howling and distressed from the difficult delivery. Joseph would have tried to wash Mary and the infant the best he could, but without clean water available, he probably had to brush away scum from the top of the trough to soak some rags in the infested water of the stable. It was not a pretty sight.

But God the Father loved you so much He was willing to let His Son endure this experience. Sure, God could have made things easier. But that was never the deal with Christ's life on earth. Yes, Jesus was both God and man, but He never used His supernatural God powers to make His human life easier. He felt pain at His birth; and He probably got hurt playing as a child. He might have been embarrassed and humiliated by other kids who taunted and ostracized Him for being conceived out of wedlock. And we know that as an adult He was often the target of slander and unwarranted accusations, leading up to His torture and crucifixion. He lived a human life, just as you and we have done, but with more severity. He endured all the pain and difficulty of humanity; none of it was minimized the least little bit by His deity.

That is both the good news and the bad news. It was bad news for Christ but good news for us. It means we have a Savior who knows what we are going through. We have a God who knows about human pain and sorrow and suffering. We have a God who can comfort us because He can sympathize with us. That is a precious gift that we often overlook when we celebrate Christmas.

❧ That first Christmas night was the birth of a King. What kind of arrangements might have been made for Mary by the townspeople of Bethlehem if they knew she was giving birth to a King?

❧ Now, try to picture the scene at the manger on that first Christmas night; not the "cleaned up" version, but the way it actually looked. Describe the conditions that existed which would have horrified any pregnant mother as she begins to give birth to her child.

❧ Remember that the composer who wrote the lyrics to "Silent Night" wasn't standing outside the stable.

❧ What do you learn about the character of God that Jesus was willing to be born in such humble circumstances and did not demand the pomp and circumstance that is appropriate for royalty?

17

GOD WITH US

"Look! The virgin will conceive a child! She will give birth to a son and will call him Immanuel (which means 'God is with us')."

ISAIAH 7:14

One of the most important—if not the most important—question anyone can ask is this: "How does God relate to the world?" If you were to ask that question in a random group of people, say at a mall or a public gathering of some kind, you would get all kinds of answers.

Some would say that God created the world, then withdrew—tht He isn't all that interested in what's going on. Others would say that God may have been powerful enough to make everything, but He certainly isn't strong enough to stop all the suffering and evil in the world. Still others would say that the question is irrelevant, because there's really no God anyway—although it's okay to believe in some sort of "cosmic power" if it helps you sleep at night.

If by chance there was someone in the crowd who really understood what the Bible says about God, and if this person was confident enough to give an answer that isn't all that popular these days, here's what you would hear: Jesus Christ.

Jesus is both the Christian answer and also the Christmas answer to the question, "How does God relate to the world?" because Jesus is God in human form. He is "the visible image of the invisible God" (Colossians 1:15). The technical term for the process of God taking on human form is *incarnation*, which comes from a Latin word meaning "taking" or "being flesh." In the Bible the concept of the incarnation is best expressed in John 1:14: "So the Word became human and made his home among us."

This verse, where Jesus is referred to as the Living Word of God, also conveys the idea that God became a human so He could come to earth and live among us. That's the essence of the name given to Jesus by the prophet Isaiah: *Immanuel*, which means "God with us." What powerful words! John MacArthur has said, "If we condense all the truths of Christmas into only three words, these would be the words."

Imagine the Creator of the universe taking on human form—the form of a baby—so that He could be with us! It's not that we're all that great to be around. We make mistakes and say the wrong things. Some of us say nasty things about God, while others prefer to think that He doesn't exist. As humans, we can be an unsavory bunch, yet the all-powerful, all-knowing, completely holy and faithful Creator of the universe willingly came in the form of a frail baby to hang out with us and show us a better way to live.

Because of Jesus, we know that God is with us. We also know that God loves us and that God is for us. Even more, because Jesus is God, we have someone who can save us—because He lived a perfect life and became the perfect sacrifice for our sins.

Because Jesus is human, He can identify with our weaknesses. We don't have to worry that God is detached from our world, not caring about us. He knows what we are going through, and He is able to help us in our distress.

During these days of Advent, the most important truth to think about is that Jesus once came in the past, He is coming again in the future, and He is here right now in the present bringing life and hope to the world.

❧ How do your beliefs about "God with us" differ from the beliefs of your neighbors or friends or perhaps some of your extended family? Do you sometimes feel like keeping your beliefs to yourself so you won't offend anyone?

❧ As a family, discuss ways you could lovingly share your belief that God sent Jesus into the world to be with us—without sounding weird or pompous.

❧ If you want to get some idea of what the responses might be to your beliefs, read John 7:5 to see what Jesus' own brothers thought of Him. Why do you think this was the case?

❧ Describe what difference it makes in your life every day to know that Jesus is always with you.

18

ANGELS

Suddenly, the angel was joined by a vast host of others—the armies of heaven— praising God and saying, "Glory to God in highest heaven, and peace on earth to those with whom God is pleased."

LUKE 2:13–14

A little snippet of the Christmas story is told in the Gospel of Matthew, but the Bible's longest narrative of Christmas events is found chapters 1 and 2 of Luke's Gospel. Not surprisingly, the writer of the Gospel of Luke was a guy named Luke. He was a Gentile Christian—a Greek by nationality—who was a friend and traveling partner of the apostle Paul.

When he wasn't researching and writing the Gospel of Luke and the book of Acts, Luke earned his living as a physician. With medical training in his background, he was naturally curious about details and wanted to get the facts correct. While he wasn't an eyewitness to Christ's birth, Bible scholars believe he personally interviewed Mary and searched for other first-hand accounts of that special night.

With his scientific background, Luke knew how to research a topic from all angles. So it's not surprising that he reports impressions from an earthly perspective—those of Mary and Joseph and the shepherds. But Luke went a step further, also reporting impressions of the first Christmas from a heavenly perspective. The human reaction was wonder and amazement, but the response of the angelic hosts was sheer joy and celebration.

The songs of praise sung by those armies of angels must have penetrated the skies for miles around. The shepherds probably covered their ears for protection from the ear-splitting volume. Had the angels hovered over a city rather than the barren Judean hillsides, residents would undoubtedly have been awakened from their sleep by the celestial anthems.

But the angelic songfest wasn't God's promotional hype to publicize the birth of His Son to everyone. He wanted to limit the announcement to a small group of shepherds, and that message was adequately handled by a single angel. (Those shepherds were "terrified" by the appearance of one angel—they were sorely impressed and received the message loud and clear. God didn't need to add angel armies to make an impact on them.)

So why all the angelic hoopla? The angels couldn't help themselves. Maybe they weren't scheduled into the program as much as they were compelled to break out in spontaneous celebration.

The whole story of the Messiah's birth took people by surprise. Mary and Joseph only had nine months to mentally prepare for it. News of the birth totally shocked the shepherds. It's understandable that the human reactions were heavily influenced by considerable confusion. But not with the angels. They knew exactly what was happening, and their celebration included a release of pent-up anticipation. They couldn't help themselves. They were exploding with excitement.

Consider that the angels probably knew of God's plan for saving the human race long before the world was created. At least from the time of Adam and Eve, the angels knew God was eventually going to send His Son to earth to be the sacrificial offering for the sins of mankind. Their comprehension of the significance of this event was much deeper and more exhaustive than the limited understanding of Mary and Joseph. The angels knew the big picture. They had been waiting thousands of years for this event to take place. They were excited that God's plan was coming to fruition; they were celebrating the enormity of Christ's love to make such a tremendous sacrifice; and they were overjoyed that all of humanity could receive the eternal benefit of what was occurring in a little barnyard lean-to in Bethlehem.

What is your excitement level when you hear the Christmas story? You enjoy an enviable vantage point similar to that of the angels: You don't suffer the limited perspective and understanding of Mary, Joseph, and the shepherds. You get the big picture. You know the significance of what happened.

Considering what God accomplished that night in Bethlehem, we should explode with praise—even if our voices aren't quite as melodious as the angel choir.

❦ Although there were no daily newspapers at the time, imagine that you were a news reporter for the *Bethlehem Gazette* at the time our Savior was born. Think of several headlines that you might suggest to your editor for the morning edition following the night of Christ's birth.

❦ Why were the angels so jubilant on the first Christmas night? What did they already know and understand that the humans in the story had not yet realized?

❦ Remember that you don't have to sing like an angel, but the Christmas season should at least put a song in your heart.

❦ Consider that the level of your excitement about the Christmas story may indicate the degree of your understanding of the miracle of the baby Jesus.

19

SHEPHERDS

That night there were shepherds staying in the fields nearby, guarding their flocks of sheep. Suddenly, an angel of the Lord appeared among them, and the radiance of the Lord's glory surrounded them.

LUKE 2:8–9

The beauty of the Christmas story is found in its simplicity—which is wrapped around intricate theology. The angel's encounter with the shepherds that first Christmas night reveals the dual aspects of commonplace humanity and majestic deity.

On the scale of occupational excitement, shepherding is probably low on the list. Oh sure, there's the occasional shooing away of a predatory animal, but an accurate fling with a sling can remedy that rather quickly. For the most part, shepherds experience the serenity of the landscape while listening to the rhythmic baas of the sheep herd. Such a job might seem nice in the abstract, but after a couple decades of living with farm animals, one might be inclined to wish for a different career. On the social scale, shepherds were not highly esteemed for their contributions. In fact, they were considered some of the dregs of society.

In this cultural context, God chose to make the greatest announcement of all time to those who were the least sophisticated. The angel didn't proclaim Jesus' birth in the temple courtyard in Jerusalem; he didn't wake the super-religious Pharisees with his declaration; and he totally bypassed the upper-class Sadducees. Instead, he went to the working-class shepherds. By doing so, the angel emphasized the utter simplicity of God's message: No snooty education or self-indulgent social status was required to understand that the Messiah had arrived. And that's why the angel declared the announcement "good news" for "all people."

So the shepherds, who had the least credibility to speak about religious issues, were the ones who brought God's message to the masses. They got the buzz started by telling everyone they could find. Ordinarily, a shepherd spouting off about theological matters might have landed himself in a padded stable pending psychiatric testing. But there was something sincere and believable about the testimony of these ragtag herders. Instead of natural skepticism, astonishment filled those who heard their message.

The shepherds were unlikely candidates for carrying such news, but they were trustworthy guys. They probably weren't shrewd enough to pull off a scam. And, unlike the Pharisees and Sadducees who often acted fraudulently prompted by ulterior motives of self-promotion, the shepherds would have no motivation for doing so. The simplicity of it all made the report believable.

There was an even deeper theological message in the angel's news flash that the shepherds overlooked. Since the Jews had been waiting centuries for their Messiah, they assumed they had proprietary ownership of Him. He was "their guy," and the changes He would institute would be for the exclusive benefit of Jews. But all Jews—shepherds, priests, and scholars alike—were clueless to one major reality: When the angel said this was "good news that will bring great joy to all people," the angel really meant all people—Gentiles as well as Jews. Hence the theological complexity.

The "all people" announced by the angel to the shepherds includes you. The Messiah was born a Jew as God had promised, and He came to bring salvation and freedom to the Jews as God had promised. But His earthly visit was a rescue mission for the rest of humanity as well.

The "good news" told to the shepherds was deceptively simple. Yes, the Messiah had arrived; that message was simple enough. But the concept that the Messiah was a Savior for all people was mind-boggling. For the first time the message of God's reconciliation extended to everyone, regardless of race or ethnicity, social background or breeding, sordid backgrounds or past failures.

The simple message the shepherds understood was good enough for them—but the rest of us can be thankful for the more complex meaning.

❦ God delights in using people we consider less deserving than ourselves. If God were to announce the birth of the Messiah in your town at this point in the 21st century, who might He choose to be His messengers? Give several reasons for your answer.

❦ The good news of the Messiah is so simple you have no excuse for not sharing it. The shepherds were eager to share the news about the birth of the Messiah, and they did so enthusiastically. Are we as eager to share this good news? If not, why not?

❦ If someone is skeptical about the message of the Messiah, we could give the advice the angel gave the shepherds: "Check it out for yourself." What are some practical ways in which we could help someone "check out" the story of Jesus?

❦ When the shepherds returned to work, they were still praising God for what they had seen and heard. Why do we stop praising God for what we've seen and heard by the time we get to our car in the church parking lot?

❦ The "good news that will bring great joy to all people," given by the angel to the shepherds, is still applicable today.

20

JOY

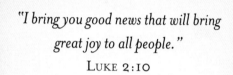

"I bring you good news that will bring great joy to all people."

LUKE 2:10

Angels are often referred to as "God's messengers" because that's what they do: They carry God's message to us humans. They aren't ordinary messengers, of course, and whenever we read about their messages and the method of delivery, we can only begin to imagine what it was like to receive a message from God via angel delivery.

When the angel brought word of Jesus' birth to the shepherds, the poor guys were scared out of their tunics. The Bible simply says they were "terrified," primarily due to the incredible "radiance of the Lord's glory" that surrounded the angelic being. Not one to let the shepherds grovel in fear, the angel reassured them by saying, "Don't be afraid! . . . I bring you good news that will bring great joy to all people." After a celestial choir concert, the shepherds, filled with the joy of the Lord, ran to see "this thing that has happened, which the Lord has told us about" (v. 15). And then they told everyone who would listen (and, we suspect, some who would not) the good news of what they had just seen.

Thus began the story of Jesus on earth. Thirty-three years later, after He had lived His remarkable life, after He was crucified and resurrected, the angel appeared again (we like to think it was the same angel, perhaps Gabriel, one of God's favorites), surrounded by the Lord's glory as before. Once again, he inspired fear among the mortals, this time two women. And as he had done with the shepherds, the angel reassured them by saying, "Don't be afraid! . . . I know you are looking for Jesus, who was crucified. He isn't here! He is risen from the dead, just as he said would happen" (Matthew 28:5–6). As the women left the angel and the empty tomb, they ran to tell others the good news of what they had seen. The Bible says, "They were very frightened but also filled with great joy" (Matthew 28:8).

Don't you find it interesting that in both of these accounts there are four elements:

❦ An angel, surrounded by God's glory, appeared to ordinary people;

❦ The people, due to the angel's glorious appearance, reacted with great fear;

❦ After being told they had nothing to be afraid of, the people were filled with great joy; and

❦ They couldn't wait to tell others what they had seen.

Like bookends on the earthly life of Christ, these parallel accounts tell us exactly how and why God has given us His joy. The *how* is pretty easy to see. God gave us His joy when He sent Jesus to be born. And then He gave us His joy again when He raised Jesus from the dead.

More perplexing is the *why*. Why would God share His joy

with those who had turned their backs on Him? For the answer, you have to go back to God's character. It is in the nature of God to love us and share Himself with us, and that includes His joy. Jesus is the absolute fullest expression of God's joy, and one of the reasons He came was to give us lives full of joy (John 10:10). When we obey Jesus and immerse ourselves in His love, He guarantees that our lives will be filled with joy. Jesus said, "Yes, your joy will overflow!" (John 15:11).

But God also gives us joy because that gives Him joy. As God's joy takes root in us, as we enjoy Him and give Him glory, the Bible says He rejoices in us with great gladness (Zephaniah 3:17).

Now there's a reason to soak up all that Christmas has to offer. It's full of joy. . . .God's joy. As we celebrate God's love for us and respond to Him in joy, the reason for the season will become incredibly meaningful for us.

❦ Think of the many ways in which "happiness" is different than "joy." (Here's an example to help you get started: Happiness is temporary; joy is everlasting.)

❦ If you've lost your joy, maybe it's because you took your eyes off of Jesus. Can you think of a time in your life when your circumstances where bleak, but you still had a spirit of God's joy within you?

❦ By its very nature, joy overflows. That's why it's impossible to keep joy to yourself. Think of some practical ways in which you can be helpful during this Advent season to someone who is in difficult circumstances. What are some acts of kindness that you can display to others? They may be encouraged by your kindness, and you are likely to experience joy in the process.

❦ Just as the darkest hour comes before dawn, your joy will often follow a time of deep sadness. Are there circumstances that you need to pray about—not only to be relieved of the difficulty—but more importantly to sense that God is in control?

21

THE WISE MEN

Jesus was born in Bethlehem in Judea,
during the reign of King Herod.
About that time some wise men from eastern
lands arrived in Jerusalem, asking,
"Where is the newborn king of the Jews?
We saw his star as it rose, and we have
come to worship him."

MATTHEW 2:1–2

A common saying at Christmastime makes an important statement: "Wise men still seek Him." The implication is that if you are wise, you will seek Jesus, just like the wise men—or magi as they are sometimes called—followed the star until they found "the newborn king of the Jews."

The story of the wise men, found only in the Gospel of Matthew, offers several lessons on what it means to truly seek Jesus today. Watch what these first-century astrologers did, and how God used them for His glory:

* The wise men were looking. At first glance, it appears these men of high position woke up one day, saw a bright star, and decided to follow it. But there's much more to the story than that. Though the Bible doesn't say much about the wise men, history tells us that they probably came from a region near the site of ancient Babylon, where reading the stars and signs was serious business. It's possible the wise men had studied the Old Testament, left by Jewish exiles centuries earlier. They might have read the prophecy, "A star will rise from Jacob" (Numbers 24:17). Armed with their knowledge of the scriptures, they were probably looking for some indication that the prophecy was true.

* God sent them a sign. A lot of people want God to send them a sign. "If You're really out there, God, show me!" The problem is that people really aren't looking for God. They want God to look for them. Not so the wise men. They were earnestly looking, so

God responded by sending them a sign—a star. Do you know that God would love to send you a sign? All you have to do is look for Him. The Bible says that God "rewards those who sincerely seek him" (Hebrews 11:6).

🌿 The wise men committed to a journey. Seeking God takes commitment. Just because God gives you a sign doesn't mean your job is done. You need to embark on a spiritual journey. You have to get out of your comfort zone and do what it takes to truly find God. That's what the wise men did. They set aside their routine, made the commitment to follow God's leading, and traveled a great distance to find the Messiah.

🌿 The wise men brought gifts. The wise men didn't begin their journey empty-handed. They brought gifts that honored Jesus. The gold was a gift fit for a king; the frankincense was a fragrance signifying deity; and the myrrh was a spice used to anoint a body for burial. The wise men probably didn't realize the true significance of their gifts, but God did. He knew that the King of kings and Lord of lords would one day lay down His life for all people. God used the wise men's gifts for His glory.

Just as the wise men opened their treasure chests and gave their gifts to the King, open your heart and give it to the Savior.

The wise men listened to God's voice. The sign God gave the wise men led them to Jesus, but God wasn't done. He spoke to them in a dream and told them to return home another way so King Herod wouldn't know where Jesus was. God still speaks today—through a still, small voice speaking through His Word, both written and living. "My sheep listen to my voice," said Jesus. "I know them, and they follow me" (John 10:27).

There's one final aspect to the wise men's story that shows us how God uses those who are obedient to Him. After the wise men returned to their homeland, God spoke to Joseph through an angel and told him that because Herod intended to kill Jesus, Joseph and Mary would need to flee to Egypt with their precious child. Historians tell us that in order to raise money for the trip, it's quite possible Joseph sold the gifts the wise men had given.

How amazing—and how comforting—to know that God always sees the big picture. He always provides for those He loves, using whatever gifts we give Him for our own benefit and His glory.

IN THE SEASON OF ADVENT

❧ Discuss as a family whether people are truly seeking
God these days, or if they are seeking what God can do
for them? Does it make any difference one way or the
other?

❧ Reflect on each of the characteristics of the wise men
in this chapter. Have each member of your family
answer these questions on a personal level:

- Are you looking for Jesus every day?
- Has God ever given you a sign? Describe what
  that was like and what you did?
- Are you committed to seeking God throughout
  your life?
- What gifts can you bring to Jesus in the
  coming year?
- In what ways can you listen to God's voice every
  day?

❧ If you haven't seen a sign from God in a while, maybe
you haven't been seeking Him.

22

THE STAR

The star they had seen in the east guided them to Bethlehem. It went ahead of them and stopped over the place where the child was. When they saw the star, they were filled with joy!

MATTHEW 2:9–10

In the hierarchy of Christmas ornaments, the position of honor goes to the one placed at the top of the tree. In most households, this distinction belongs to. . .drum roll, please. . ."the star." ("The angel" comes in a distant second as the most popular tree-topper, and there are no serious contenders after that.)

How did the star earn such a privileged position in Christmas decorating schemes? After all, in the historical account of the first Christmas, the star doesn't have lead billing. It's not mentioned in the Christmas account as reported in Luke's Gospel; you'll only find it mentioned in the book of Matthew—and even there it gets only a brief reference in four verses (chapter 2, verses 2, 7, 9, and 10).

What do we know—or not know—about this famous star?

❦ It was noticed by the wise men who lived far away in the East. But the shepherds in the hills outside Bethlehem apparently didn't see it. (They saw angels but had to run around the back alleys of Bethlehem seeking a makeshift delivery room in a stable.) Apparently, there was no huge star suspended a few feet above the stable as is often depicted in paintings and in that nativity scene your kid made out of Popsicle sticks.

❦ The star announced and publicized the birth of the Savior to those wise men, and based on their study of the Old Testament, they journeyed to Jerusalem to make further inquiry. After consultation with the sages in King Herod's court, it was determined that Bethlehem would be the Messiah's birthplace according to the ancient prophets. As soon as the wise men resumed their trek, now headed toward Bethlehem, the star appeared to them again. It "went ahead of them" on the way to Bethlehem. Since quite awhile had passed between the initial appearance of the star and the wise men's journey to Jerusalem, Jesus and His parents were no longer in the stable. They were most likely settled into some temporary housing. The star must have had accurate GPS capabilities, because the wise men didn't have to knock on every door in the neighborhood. The star actually "stopped over the place where the child was."

Astronomers have long speculated about the nature of the star. Was that first sighting an unidentified comet? Maybe it was the alignment of Jupiter, Saturn, and Mars that occurred in 6 BC. Or maybe there were two stars: The first could have been an anomaly in the constellations, noticed by astronomers as a special occurrence, which would have meaning to anyone studying the scriptures and looking for hints as to the arrival of the Messiah. The second could have been a star that, with pinpoint accuracy, could identify a specific house in a Google map-like fashion, but was only visible to the wise men—so as not to reveal the baby's location to King Herod.

The Bible is not a science textbook. For example, it refers to God as a Shepherd, revealing details about His character—but it doesn't tell us how to clone a sheep. So the lack of a scientific explanation of the star of Bethlehem should cause us no concern.

In nontechnical and nontheoretical language, the Bible tells it like it happened: God used a star in the sky to proclaim to the wise men that the Messiah had arrived. Later, God used a star to miraculously lead the wise men to the very house in which Mary, Joseph, and the baby Jesus were living. When viewed in this context, the star is simply one of many circumstances that illustrate God's intricate plan.

And maybe that's what the star on your tree should represent: something to draw your attention to God's involvement in Christmas. He invented the holiday, you know.

❧ Whether you place a star or an angel on the top of your Christmas tree, make a special occasion out of it. Recite the facts of how the star/angel fits into the story of the first Christmas. After you place the symbol atop your tree, say a prayer to God, thanking Him for this tangible prop that will remind you of Christ's birth whenever you look at your Christmas tree.

❧ The wise men were first attracted by the star. Later, after following the star, they found and worshiped the child who came to be the Light of the World. To what do you look for guidance when you want to encounter God? How do you go about finding Him? Although the wise men could look for the Messiah's announcement in the sky, you'll find it easier simply to read the New Testament. Begin a habit of reading one of the Gospels (Matthew, Mark, Luke, or John) during the Advent Season. These biographies of the life of Christ will surely cause you to encounter Him.

❧ God isn't interested in playing hide-and-seek. He wants you to find Him. And He will make Himself obvious if you just start looking.

23

THE NATIVITY

*Christmas is the gentlest,
loveliest festival of the revolving year—
and yet, for all that,
when it speaks, its voice
has strong authority.*

W. J. CAMERON

The nativity is one of the best-known, most often told stories in history. Asked to describe the events surrounding Jesus' birth, most people could probably give the basic components of the story: An angel tells a young virgin she's going to give birth to the Savior of the world. . . . Mary and Joseph travel to Bethlehem, but there's no room in the inn. . . . They find shelter in a stable where Jesus is born. . . . Angels announce the good news to a bunch of shepherds, who run to see the baby Jesus. . . . Some wise men drop by to pay their respects and leave some gifts. That's the nativity story in a nutshell—at least the one you'll see at your church's Christmas pageant, featuring children in bathrobes and fake beards.

As much we enjoy those charming pageants, we think those annual presentations sell the Christmas story short. Reducing God's great epic to a single stage with amateur actors and homemade props can't begin to capture its scope and grandeur. Truth is, the nativity is a massive and earth-shattering event that spans the unlimited time and space of eternity, featuring characters both visible and invisible. It's so grand and so powerful that any attempt—whether a church play or a Hollywood blockbuster—fails to express what it means for God to relate to His human creation the way He did.

The plot itself is one for the ages, full of paradoxes and reversals. The tiny baby born on earth is actually a heavenly King. The birth is in the lowliest of places, and the human characters God recruits are humble people without status. Except for the wise men (who came two years after Christ's birth), those who take part in the story and then share it with others are from the bottom strata of society.

The greatest human writer could never invent such a wondrous story. It came to us directly from the mind of God, who through the nativity announced several truths to the world:

- The weak will be made strong;

- The lowly will be exalted;

- The poor in spirit will become spiritually rich;

- Those who mourn will be comforted;

- Those who are meek will inherit the earth; and

- Those who desire a truly good life will find it.

And it's all because Jesus came to the world on that first Christmas.

This is the heart of the nativity. It's a mystery revealed by God, centered in Christ, put into effect when the time was right. It's a story for the ages, not something to observe like an audience watches a play—we can actually jump in ourselves, as characters with the opportunity to participate in all that the story means.

So the next time you see a nativity pageant in church, or as you talk about the nativity during this Advent season, view it with this fresh perspective. Put yourself in the tableau, because God didn't write the story for just anyone. When it's all said and done, He did it for you.

❧ Here's a fun assignment that's going to take some time, but the outcome will be worth the effort. Produce a nativity play with your family members as the characters! You could use the Christmas story as told in the Gospel of Luke as the narration (set pieces are optional), but feel free to write some lines for your characters. What do you think Mary, Joseph, the shepherds, and the wise men would say? What emotions would they express? You might be surprised how your family will feel after rehearsing and performing your original nativity play.

❧ At the very least, tell the nativity story to your family. Be dramatic! After all, it isn't a fairy tale—this is God's great story.

❧ Be thankful that God uses the lowly to accomplish His purposes, because in comparison to His greatness, we are all lowly.

24

GIFTS AND GIVING

Probably the reason we all go so haywire
at Christmastime with the endless
unrestrained and often silly buying of gifts
is that we don't quite know
how to put our love into words.
HARLAN MILLER

The tradition of Christmastime gift giving didn't begin when Jesus was born. Mary and Joseph may have marked the occasion of Christ's first birthday, but it wasn't celebrated with a gift exchange among the relatives and neighbors. The entire Christmas gift thing came hundreds of years later—and it probably wasn't rooted in the Christian faith. But we can still attach a spiritual significance to our own customs of giving and receiving gifts at Christmastime.

God gave the gift of His Son to all humanity that first Christmas evening. In doing so, He established three principles of gift giving that provide good guidelines for us to follow:

❧   **The gift was exactly what we needed.** One technical term describes a Christmas gift that nobody wants: fruitcake. But the category also includes Aunt Kim's gift of souvenir ashtrays to her nonsmoking niece and nephew; a necktie for Grandpa who only wears polyester jogging suits; and the box of See's candy you gave your pastor's wife, not knowing she was diabetic. God's gift, though, was specifically and uniquely what the human race needed—it was a gift designed and intended to cure our sin virus. God could have given other nice gifts (like heat without humidity or broccoli that tastes like chocolate), but anything less than a sacrifice for our sins would have left us in desperate need.

❦ **The gift wasn't what we were expecting.** Often, a gift may meet a need, though it isn't what the recipient was hoping for. Just ask any teenager who gets socks for Christmas. Sure, you need things like socks and toilet paper, but no one puts them on their Christmas list. The same is true of the Jews in the first century (and all of humanity since, for that matter). They wanted a Messiah who would free them from Roman oppression, leading them into autonomy and prosperity. They weren't expecting a Messiah who would speak about the spiritual freedom that comes from an intimate relationship with God. That's exactly what those first-century Jews needed, but they had other things higher on their list. Still, God gave them what He knew would be best for them.

❦ **A sacrifice was involved.** There may be nothing more disappointing on Christmas morning than receiving a gift that reveals a lack of effort on the part of the giver. Just ask a wife whose husband presents a stapled-shut bag from the Gas-N-Go; inside she finds a tin of breath mints, an assortment of candy bars, windshield wiper replacement blades, and an incriminating receipt indicating the purchase was made twenty-

seven minutes earlier. In contrast, the most
meaningful gifts are those that involve an obvious
sacrifice by the giver. Balmy weather and candy-
flavored vegetables would have been easy for
God to conjure up. Such gifts might have been
enjoyed by humanity, but the gifts would not
have involved even the slightest inconvenience on
God's part. Instead, He chose to send His Son to
earth, knowing that Christ would be tortured and
put to a brutal death. As the Bible says, "There
is no greater love than to lay down one's life for
one's friends" (John 15:13).

As you make your Christmas-shopping decisions, keep these
principles in mind. Let your love for the recipient be reflected
by a gift that is uniquely appropriate for that person. Give a
gift that shows you made a sacrifice, not necessarily in money
but in effort and thoughtfulness. And, whatever you do, don't
Christmas shop at the Gas-N-Go.

❦ The statement is true: It is not the gift but the thought that counts. But it's also true that the gift usually reflects the amount of thought that was involved. Use the Advent season to pray for those you remember at Christmas time. Prayers on their behalf may be the greatest gift you can give to them. When you give tangible gifts, include a card on which you can mention that you are praying for them.

❦ A gift of your time and attention is more valuable than anything that can be wrapped.

❦ The cost of a gift is irrelevant if the gift was thoughtfully chosen. A high price is meaningless if there was little thought involved.

❦ You've given a good gift if it conveys how well you know the recipient.

❦ Remember that your appreciation is the gift you give back in return for a gift you have received.

25

RECEIVING

Yet to all who did receive him, to those who believed in his name, he gave the right to become children of God.

JOHN 1:12 NIV

Christmas is the season of giving. No one needs to tell you that, because this time of year every store and nearly every media outlet reminds you constantly that it's time to shop for gifts. And if you happen to miss the commercial clues, some of your closest friends and family members are more than happy to provide you with a list of suggested items they would love to receive.

You probably don't mind those attempts to inspire your giving. The old saying, "It's better to give than to receive," really is true. Giving is fun. Giving is fulfilling. What isn't as fulfilling is receiving gifts. That's not to say it isn't enjoyable, because it is. Opening presents is a blast, but our enthusiasm for what lies beneath the wrapping paper can quickly die, usually for one of two reasons.

First, the gift can turn out to be much less than you thought it would be. If this happens, it's important to maintain your cheery mood, even though you've just received a pair of oven mitts from Aunt Rose. Secondly, enthusiasm can also wane when you get a gift that goes way beyond what you expected—especially if you were "exchanging" gifts with another person. Elation can quickly turn to embarrassment, even resentment, if the gift puts you in an awkward position, such as feeling like you don't deserve it.

The point is this: Not only is it better to give than to receive, it's also easier. Receiving something—especially something you don't think you deserve—can be tough.

Perhaps you already know where we're going with this. It's one thing to receive a valuable earthly gift for which you feel unworthy. Imagine what it's like to receive a gift from heaven—a good and perfect gift—whose value is beyond measure. That's exactly what God asks us to do at Christmas, when we are reminded that He has given us the greatest gift of all, the gift of His Son. And just as an earthly gift can't be earned (otherwise it would be more like a bonus than a gift), neither can God's heavenly gift. It must be received.

Makes sense, doesn't it? At Christmas, what good is a gift left under the tree, unopened? It's pretty to look at, but it doesn't do any good. Only when you open and receive the gift does it serve the purpose for which it was intended.

Think about God's gift of Jesus for a minute. Have you "unwrapped" and received the Gift? Or have you left Him wrapped and lying in the manger, waiting for Christmas to pass so you can put Him away for another year? The apostle John, reflecting on the fact that Jesus was born into a world that did not receive Him, made the observation that anyone who receives the gift of life through God's Son will gain the right to become God's children—in effect adopted into God's eternal family as co-heirs with Christ.

There's nothing we could possibly do to be worthy of receiving God's great gift—it's based completely on His grace. But receive it we must, and what better time than Christmas?

- Ask each family member to describe the best gift they ever received at Christmas. What happened to the gift? Do they still have it? What does this say about the fleeting value of earthly gifts?

- Now ask each family member to describe the best gift they have ever given at Christmas. What kind of thought and preparation went into selecting or making the gift, and then wrapping it for the special occasion? What was it like to watch the person open the gift?

- Have those family members who have received God's eternal love gift of Jesus talk about their experience. What difference has the gift made in their lives?

- There's nothing more disappointing to a gift-giver than to know the gift was never received and opened. Imagine how God feels when people refuse to receive and open the gift of His Son.

26

FORGIVENESS

Every time you see the manger,
you should remember the cross.

In an earlier chapter we made the point that love is the reason we have Christmas. Now let's consider the result of Christmas. Love motivated God to send Jesus that first Christmas night. But as important as love is, it doesn't tell us everything about Jesus and why He came to earth in the first place.

"God so loved the world that he gave his one and only Son" (John 3:16 NIV). That's the reason Jesus came to earth. But it's only one part of the story. The other part is the result of that love: "That whoever believes in him will not perish but have eternal life." In a word, the result of the love and the result of the story of Jesus is forgiveness—because that's what happens when we believe in God's Son. We are forgiven.

Early in the ministry of Jesus a paralyzed man was brought to Him for healing. The people who brought the man believed Jesus could heal their friend, and, because of their faith, Jesus did heal him—but not before He forgave the man of his sins. You see, the man's body wasn't the only thing that was paralyzed. His spirit was, too. That was the issue that concerned Jesus the most. Physical healing is for this life only, but spiritual healing is for eternity.

In more ways than one, we are like that paralyzed man. We come to Jesus thinking that our physical (or emotional) hurts are the big issue, but Jesus has something more to offer. He offers forgiveness. He promises forgiveness. Yes, Jesus wants to heal our hurts, but first He wants to forgive us. Without forgiveness (the result of Christmas) we cannot fully experience the love of God (the reason for Christmas).

Someone has said that the life of Jesus began in a stable and ended on a cross. During this season of joy and love and peace and goodwill, it isn't exactly pleasant to think that the baby in the manger will grow up to suffer and die. Why does the Christmas story have to end that way? Because the cross is what makes Jesus' promise to forgive a reality. The truth is that the manger and the cross are both integrally related. Without the birth of Jesus, there is no love. But without the cross, there is no forgiveness.

There's another dimension to forgiveness that will help you experience Christmas more fully. Just as God has forgiven you because of Jesus, you need to forgive others. There's no better time than now to think about those people who have offended you or harmed you in some way. Are you holding a grudge or cherishing bitterness toward anyone else? In the spirit of Christmas, where love and forgiveness stand like bookends on either end of the remarkable life of Jesus, you need to forgive.

Whenever we're tempted to be stingy with our forgiveness, we need to remember that in our relationship with God, we are the offenders and God is the offended. We have hurt God and don't deserve His forgiveness—but He made the first move toward us. Out of His deep love for us, through the death of Jesus, He forgives us—and He expects us to forgive others.

❀ Without forgiveness, there can be no healing. There are likely to have been people in your past who hurt you deeply. Have you forgiven them, truly forgiven them, to the point where the former hurt is no longer an issue? If not, then talk to God about this. Ask Him to help you forgive them.

❀ Without forgiveness, there can be no love. Do you need to ask someone to forgive you for an unloving action on your part? Don't let this Advent season pass without you communicating your apology and a request for forgiveness. (Whether or not they agree to forgive you is not as important as your need to make the request.)

❀ Without forgiveness, there is only the manger. Thank God often that He has forgiven you because of Christ's act of supreme love on the Cross.

❀ The journey from the stable to the cross isn't an easy one, but it's a journey we must take.

27

PEACE

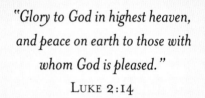

"Glory to God in highest heaven,
and peace on earth to those with
whom God is pleased."

LUKE 2:14

There's a lot of talk about peace at Christmas. Even those who don't care much about Christmas as a celebration of Jesus' birth like to promote peace at this time of year. You could say that Christmas is the season of peace for the whole world.

Of course, if the newspaper headlines are any indication, there's not much peace going on in the world, whether it's across the seas, across the country, or in your own town. It may be Christmas on the calendar, but bombings, murders, kidnappings, domestic violence, racism, and all sorts of bad stuff are still happening everywhere you look. Even if you don't focus on the violence, you find arguments, strife, and disharmony in your workplace, your neighborhood, maybe even your home.

So what's all this "peace on earth" business the angels announced that first Christmas? Was it all hype? If there would never be peace in the world, why did the prophet Isaiah give God's Son the title "Prince of Peace" and predict that "His government and its peace will never end" (Isaiah 9:6–7)?

For the answer, take a look at the entire announcement the angels gave that holy night:

> *"Glory to God in highest heaven, and peace on earth to those with whom God is pleased."*
> LUKE 2:14

It isn't peace for the whole world, but only for those God

favors—in other words, those who have put their trust in Jesus and committed themselves to Him. Jesus explained the nature of this peace when He told His followers, "'I am leaving you with a gift—peace of mind and heart. And the peace I give is a gift the world cannot give. So don't be troubled or afraid'" (John 14:27).

This kind of internal serenity transcends the external peace everyone hopes for at Christmas. Though the storms of life rage around us, we can have calm assurance that our mighty and loving God has us firmly in His hand—if we have a personal relationship with the One who came to bring peace to the world.

This also explains Isaiah's prophecy about a "government and its peace" that will never end. All those who put their trust in Jesus become part of His spiritual kingdom—His government—where Jesus is not only Savior, but also Lord. This peaceable kingdom ever expands as more and more people discover God's good news for themselves.

Meanwhile, as Christ's followers, we are to do all we can to bring peace—both spiritual and physical—to the world, especially during this season of Advent. The Bible tells us, "Do all that you can to live in peace with everyone" (Romans 12:18). Of all the people in the world, those with God's peace in their hearts should be the most intentional about promoting peace. Just like the angels, we should proclaim and embody peace on earth, because we are the ones upon whom God's favor rests. It's both our privilege and our responsibility.

❧ Talk as a family about peace and what you can do in your own home to live more peacefully with each other. How can you resolve differences in a more peaceful manner?

❧ Now talk about your community and the country. Why is peace so hard to achieve? Make a list of three things your family could do in the coming year to encourage others to live more peacefully.

❧ What is the difference between peace with God and the peace of God? Is it possible to have both? How?

❧ Jesus is the "Prince of Peace" in every way: He brings peace to all who follow Him, and someday He will bring peace to the world.

28

GO TELL IT

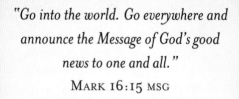

"Go into the world. Go everywhere and announce the Message of God's good news to one and all."

MARK 16:15 MSG

From the moment Jesus was born, a whole bunch of people (and more than a few angels) were singing His praises—and they haven't stopped since. As you've read through this book, we hope you've learned why that's the case. We also hope that you have opened your heart to Jesus as you anticipate His arrival. The waiting is almost over!

The birth of Jesus that first Christmas wasn't just any birth, because Jesus wasn't just any person. He was God in human form, sent to earth by His heavenly Father so that God could establish a personal and eternal relationship with anyone who would receive the gift of His Son. That's the good news of Christmas. Indeed, it's the good news of the Bible.

Something about good news makes it impossible to keep it to yourself. When you discover something that changes your life, you are compelled to share it with others. That's what happened that first Christmas night. The first to tell others about Jesus were the angels. They made a big announcement to the shepherds, who in turn ran all around Bethlehem telling people what they had seen and heard. (We suspect they caused quite a ruckus, being shepherds and all.) Later, the wise men came to see Jesus, and undoubtedly told everyone back in their homeland what they had seen.

All kinds of people—from common laborers to people of high standing—were engaged in telling others that Jesus Christ was born. How appropriate! You see, Jesus didn't come for certain kinds of people—He came for everyone. Throughout His life on earth, Jesus touched every kind of person: poor and rich, young and old, Jew and Gentile, woman and man, ruler and oppressed. And when He left earth to return to His heavenly home, He told His followers to continue His work—by going everywhere to tell everyone the message of God's good news.

Jesus may have been born two thousand years ago, but His presence is just as real today as it was when He physically walked the earth. He is still touching lives, still changing hearts. The song the angels sang on that first Christmas night can be your song, too. Don't be afraid to let your light shine. A dark and hurting world needs the light of Jesus now more than ever.

Go, tell it on the mountain,
Over the hills and everywhere
Go, tell it on the mountain,
That Jesus Christ is born.

❧ How was your Christmas season different this year than other years because your family focused on Advent? Have each family member describe the ways Advent made a difference in their life.

❧ Think of a family you know that celebrates Christmas but not the Christ of Christmas. How would you describe your Advent experience to this family (without making them feel uncomfortable of course)?

❧ It's one thing to tell about Jesus with your words. It's much better to tell about Him with your life.

❧ Let the shepherds be your example. They didn't have any theological credentials. They just told people about their personal encounter with Christ.

About Bruce and Stan

Bruce and Stan have co-authored more than sixty books about the Christian faith, including bestsellers such as *God Is in the Small Stuff—and it all matters*. They are passionate about presenting the truth of God in a manner that is clear, casual, and correct.

When Bruce Bickel didn't make the cut as a stand-up comedian, he became a lawyer, which is a career in which he's considered hilarious. He is active in church ministries and currently serves on the Board of Westmont College. He lives in Central California with his wife, where kids and grandkids surround them.

Stan Jantz has been involved with content throughout his professional career as a bookseller, publisher, and writer. He resides with his wife in Southern California, where he serves on the board of trustees of Biola University.

If you have any questions, comments, or just want to share a story, contact Bruce and Stan at info@conversantlife.com.